A Little Dutch Cookbook

voor Saskia
Liefs van
Sint & Piet

Karen Sluiters

ILLUSTRATED BY DITTE KUMMER

Chronicle Books

First published in 1992 by
The Appletree Press Ltd,
7 James Street South, Belfast BT2 8DL.

First published in the United States in 1990 by
Chronicle Books, 275 Fifth Street,
San Francisco, CA 94103

ISBN: 0-8118-0168-3

9 8 7 6 5 4 3 2 1

Introduction

Holland's countryside, with its open spaces and flat scenery, crossed by canals, wide rivers and tree-lined roads, gives visitors a sense of tranquillity which is in stark contrast to the hustle and bustle of the cities. The countryside provides rich produce: cheese, meat, poultry and a great variety of vegetables. Holland's seas and dykes provide many species of fish and seafood for dishes such as Stewed Eels and Mussels with Cheese. All of these foods are displayed in abundance in the markets of many Dutch towns. The Dutch have healthy appetites and this shows in their traditional recipes. These recipes, some several hundred years old, have come down from mother to daughter. They are very nutritious and economical. This is a collection of my favorite dishes. I hope they give you as much pleasure as they have given me. *Eet smakelijk! Bon Appetit!* Good eating!

A note on measures

Spoon measurements are level except where otherwise indicated. Seasonings can of course be adjusted according to taste. Recipes are for four.

Krentenbollen

Currant Buns

These buns were a treat when I was a young child. It was wonderful to wake up to the smell of baking on a Sunday morning and to come down to breakfast just in time to see my mother take the buns from the oven. They are delicious served with unsalted creamy butter or, even better, eaten with mature Dutch Gouda cheese.

---

2 cups plain flour
$^1/_2$ oz dried yeast
good pinch salt
2 tbsp superfine sugar
1 egg
$^1/_2$ cup lukewarm milk
2 tbsp melted butter
1 cup currants
(makes 8 buns)

Sift the flour in a large bowl and mix in the salt and superfine sugar. Make a well in the center and add half of the egg. Mix the yeast with 5 tbsp of the warm milk in a small bowl and pour it in the mixture. Add the rest of the milk with the melted butter and knead into a smooth dough. Cover the bowl with a tea towel and leave the mixture to rise in a warm place for about $^3/_4$ hour. Knead in the currants. Divide the dough into 8 buns, place on a greased baking tray and leave to rise for another $^1/_2$ hour. Before baking, brush the buns with the

remainder of the egg. Bake for 15 to 20 minutes in the middle of a fairly hot oven at 400°F until golden brown.

Fries Suikerbrood

Frisian Sugarloaf

This sweet bread is from the northern province of Friesland. Slices of the bread, liberally spread with creamy, unsalted butter, were traditionally served with coffee made in a special Frisian pewter pot to guests, in the parlor, after church.

---

3 ¹/₂ cups plain flour
¹/₂ oz dried yeast
1 cup lukewarm milk
1 tsp granulated sugar
pinch salt
1 cup crushed sugar lumps
2 tsp cinnamon

Make a thick yeast dough with the flour, yeast, 1 tsp sugar and half of the milk in a large bowl (see method on page 4). Leave the bowl in a warm place, covered by a tea towel, for ¹/₂ hour. Add the remainder of the milk, a pinch of salt and stir. Add the crushed sugar lumps and the cinnamon. Knead the dough until it comes easy from the hands. Cover the bowl and leave the mixture to rise for the second time on a warm place for 1 hour. Grease a 12 inch long bread pan and fill with the dough. Bake the bread on the bottom rack of a very hot oven at 475°F for about 45 minutes. Remove from oven and allow to cool.

Vleeskroketten

Meat Croquettes

This favorite snack can be bought everywhere in Holland from automatic food-machines — as the Amsterdammers say, "out of the wall". In restaurants and cafés they are served for lunch on white bread with *Zoetzuur* (see page 43) and sharp mustard on the side. You can use beef, veal or chicken meat.

2 tbsp butter	pepper and salt
I tbsp plain flour	sprig parsley, chopped
I 3/4 cups stock	pinch curry powder
1/2 lb cooked beef, veal	toasted bread-crumbs
or chicken, finely chopped	I beaten egg
I small onion, finely chopped	oil for deep-frying

(makes 4 croquettes)

Melt the butter and stir in the flour to make a smooth roux. Slowly add the stock and keep stirring for 10 minutes until the sauce is cooked. Lightly fry the onion and stir it and the chopped meat into the sauce. Add the salt, pepper, curry and parsley to taste. Spread this mixture on a plate to cool and stiffen. Divide the mixture into 4 equal parts and make into oblongs with the help of two spoons. Roll the croquettes in the bread-crumbs, then egg, and again in bread-crumbs, taking care that the sides are covered as well. Deep-fry the croquettes in hot oil 350°F for about 4 minutes. Serve with pickles and mustard.

Spekpannekoek

Bacon Pancake

In almost every tourist resort in Holland one can find a "Pannekoekenhuis", or pancake house, where only pancakes are served. My recollection is that the pancakes served are so enormous that they hang over the edge of the plate. The *Spekpannekoek* is an old-fashioned type of savory pancake.

---

1 cup plain flour
1 cup buckwheat flour
1 tsp salt
1 egg
1 oz dried yeast
3 3/4 cups lukewarm milk
1/2 lb thinly sliced streaky bacon
stroop *or syrup to serve*
(makes 8 pancakes)

Mix both flours with the salt in a bowl. Make a well in the center and add the egg. Mix the yeast with some of the lukewarm milk and add to the mixture. Stirring from the center, gradually add 1 3/4 cups of the milk. Stir until bubbles appear then add the remainder of the milk. Cover the bowl with a tea towel and leave the mixture to rise for 1 1/2 hours on a warm place.

Fry three slices of the bacon in the frying pan until light brown then add some of the batter, swirling it so that the bacon and the base of the pan are well covered. Cook the pancake until golden brown on each side. Serve it with *stroop* (a special Dutch syrup) or substitute maple or golden syrup.

Hengstenpap

Stallion Soup

It is said that this soup has aphrodisiac properties. *Hengstenpap*, a very old soup dish from the province of Groningen, is traditionally served at weddings. This recipe was given to me by the chef of 't Schathoes, a restaurant in Menkemaborg. When I asked why it was called *Hengstenpap*, I was told it "had a real kick in it". In fact, it is a strong, spicy, nutritious, thick vegetable soup. What makes this soup so delicious is the amount and variety of vegetables. It is served with brown bread, rye bread or pumpernickel.

3 leeks	10 cups strong beef stock
4 medium carrots	2 tbsp pearl barley
1/4 medium cauliflower	2 tsp grated ginger-root
8 oz mushrooms	salt and pepper
1 cup peas	2 oz minced beef
1/2 or 1 small celeriac	1 tbsp toasted bread-crumbs
3 large sprigs parsley	1 egg

Clean the vegetables. Cut the leeks and carrots in rings, slice the mushrooms, cut the cauliflower into little flowerets, dice the celeriac and sprinkle with lemon juice to prevent discoloring, chop the parsley. Add all the vegetables to the stock together with the grated ginger-root and pearl barley. Bring to a boil and simmer for 50 minutes. Add salt to taste. Mix the minced beef with the toasted bread-crumbs, salt and pepper. With wet hands roll into little balls and add to the soup. Cook for

another 10 minutes. At the last minute add the beaten egg by pouring it through a sieve and swirling it in the soup.

Grootmoeders Kruudsoep

Grandmama's Herbal Soup

This is a lovely delicate soup which is delicious as a starter at a dinner party. If you can find it, use fresh chervil for this soup. Other herbs or vegetables can be used instead — for example, parsley, spinach, leeks or white cabbage.

---

1 onion, finely chopped
$^{1}/_{2}$ cup chervil, finely chopped
2 tbsp butter
2 tbsp plain flour
5 cups chicken stock, heated
4 tbsp cream
salt and pepper
lemon juice (to taste)

Melt the butter and gently cook the onion and the chervil until the onion is soft but not colored. Sprinkle the flour over this mixture and add the heated stock slowly while stirring all the time. Mix the sour cream with some of the hot stock before adding it at the last minute to the soup. Take the pan from the heat and add salt, pepper and lemon juice to taste. Serve the soup with small triangles of toasted white bread or melba toast.

Erwtensoep

Pea Soup

Erwtensoep or *snert*, as it is popularly called, is one of Holland's best known national dishes. The Dutch are keen soup eaters and this one never goes amiss on cold wintery days when the ground is covered with snow and the canals are frozen over. This soup is very filling and is eaten as a main meal. *Erwtensoep* is best served with brown bread and is even better the next day.

---

2 cups dried green split peas
I lb round end leg of pork
$^1/_2$ lb smoked bacon
5 medium-size onions
I large carrot
$^1/_2$ or I small celeriac
2 leeks
4 tbsp celery leaves
salt and pepper
2 medium-size potatoes
(serves six)

Soak the peas overnight in 8 cups of water. Clean the vegetables and chop them finely. Cook the peas gently in their soaking water together with the pork, smoked bacon, onions, carrot, celeriac and leeks for 1½ hours. Add pepper, salt and potatoes and cook for another 20 minutes. Remove the pork and smoked bacon, cut them into small pieces, and return to the soup. At the last moment, stir in the finely-chopped celery leaves.

Mosselen met Kaas

Mussels with Cheese

Mussels are a favorite in Dutch households and they can be found on the menu in most restaurants. *Mosselen met kaas* is a lunch dish usually served with a green salad.

---

2 lb fresh mussels
I onion, finely chopped
I leek, finely sliced
I carrot, finely sliced
2 sprigs parsley, finely chopped
8 oz tomatoes
4 oz Gouda cheese, grated
parsley to garnish

Clean the mussels in cold water and discard any that are open. Mix the vegetables with the parsley and put in a wide saucepan. Add a little water and place the mussels on top. Cover the saucepan. Steam the mussels on a medium heat for about 3 minutes. When the shells are open, remove the saucepan from the heat and drain, discarding any mussels that remain closed. When cool, remove the mussels from their shells. Discard half the shells and beards from the mussels. Skin the tomatoes, remove the pips and chop the fleshy part finely. Place each mussel in one half of a shell and arrange on a dish. Blend the chopped tomatoes and grated cheese. Spread the tomato mixture over the mussels and brown under the grill. Garnish with parsley.

Vijfschaft

Five in One

Brown or pinto beans have always been a staple food in Holland, especially in the winter months. Here is one of the many traditional, nourishing main dishes which includes them. It's a one-pot dinner. The "five" in the title stands for the five vegetables and fruit — beans, onions, carrots, potatoes and apples.

---

1 cup pinto beans
1 cup carrots, chopped
1 cup sliced onion
salt and pepper
³/₄ lb peeled potatoes, cubed
8 oz smoked bacon
8 oz Gelderse rookworst *(Dutch smoked sausage)*
2 cooking apples, sliced
pat of butter

Soak the beans overnight in 8 cups of water then boil for 1 hour in a large saucepan in the same water. Add, in this order, carrots, onion rings, salt and pepper, potatoes, smoked bacon, and smoked sausage. Cook covered for about 15 minutes on a medium heat. Add the apples and cook for another 10 minutes. When the *Vijfschaft* is ready, remove the smoked bacon and smoked sausage and cut into small pieces. Return the meat to the saucepan, add a pat of butter and carefully stir it in. Serve with a green salad.

Schelvis met Mosterdsaus

Haddock in Mustard Sauce

When I visit friends in Holland I can expect to eat fish at least once. There's a great variety of fish and many dishes to choose from. Haddock and cod are two of the fish regularly found on the menu. Both can be used for this recipe.

---

2 lb haddock, filleted

Court-bouillon	Mustard Sauce
8 cups water	*2 cups court-bouillon*
1/2 cup dry white wine	*1 1/2 tbsp plain flour*
1 large carrot	*3 tbsp butter*
1 large onion	*1 big tbsp Dijon mustard*
2 sprigs parsley	
1 bayleaf	
10 white peppercorns, crushed	
salt	

Prepare the *court-bouillon* by simmering all the ingredients together for 1 hour. Strain the liquid into another pan and place the fish in it. Slowly simmer until the fish is cooked. Remove the fish and keep warm on a hot plate. Make the sauce by melting the butter and stirring in the flour to make a smooth roux. Slowly add the *court-bouillon* and stir until the sauce thickens. Stir in mustard. Serve the sauce on the fish or separately in a sauce-boat, with boiled new potatoes and baby carrots.

Zeeuws Gestoofde Paling

Stewed Eel

There are many ways to cook eel but my grandmother from Zeeland made the best eel dish I've ever had. It is very simple and absolutely delicious. The eel used for this dish is the fresh-water eel and should be not more than 1 inch thick.

---

4 lb eel
10 fresh sage leaves
1/2 tsp salt
butter

Ask the fish dealer to clean the eels, strip them of their skins, and cut them in pieces of about 2 inches. Wash and drain in a colander. Sprinkle with salt. Grease an ovenproof dish with butter and place the eel pieces upright, side by side, in it. Add about 1–2 tbsp water. Sprinkle the sage over the eels. Stew in the middle of a pre-heated oven at 400°F for 25–30 minutes. The flesh should just about fall off the bone. Serve with boiled potatoes and a salad, or with sweet apple sauce.

Hachée

Meat Stew

I have had *Hachée* many times on cold winter evenings. It is a lovely sweet-and-sour meat stew and easy to make. It can be eaten in the summer as well but is served then on rice with a green salad. The trick of this dish is to let the onions brown which makes them sweeter.

1 lb rib steak
3 large onions
6 tbsp butter
1/2 cup plain flour
2 bayleaves
4 white peppercorns, crushed
2 whole cloves
1 tsp sugar, heaped
3 cups beef stock
2 tbsp red wine vinegar
salt and pepper

Cut the meat into chunks and season. Peel the onions and slice them in rings. Heat the butter in a saucepan and brown both onions and meat. Sprinkle the flour over this mixture and stir until the flour is light brown in color. Add the herbs, sugar, stock and vinegar and leave the stew on a low heat in the tightly-covered pan for 1 1/2 hours or until the meat is tender. Serve *Hachée* with boiled potatoes and red cabbage.

Kip in 't Pannetje

Chicken in the Pot

In spring this is *the* Sunday lunch. Everything is cooked in the same big pot. It's wonderful. Try it!

---

1 chicken about 2 lb
white pepper and salt
6 tbsp butter
15–20 small new potatoes
1 large carrot, diced or 12 baby carrots
12 whole shallots or small onions
8 oz button mushrooms, sliced
$\frac{1}{2}$ cup dry white wine, warmed
5 oz bacon, diced
1 tbsp finely-chopped parsley

Sprinkle a little salt and lots of white pepper inside the chicken. Melt the butter and brown the chicken in a large pan on a medium heat. Remove the chicken and keep warm on a hot plate. Fry the potatoes, carrots and shallots in the same butter until golden. Add the mushrooms and the warmed white wine. Place the chicken on top of the vegetables. Season again. Cover the pan and leave to simmer on a low heat for 1 hour. Fry the bacon until crisp. When it is cooked, take the chicken from the pan. Mix the bacon through the vegetables and transfer into a heated deep serving dish. Put the chicken on the vegetable mixture and sprinkle with finely-chopped parsley.

Leidse Hutspot

Leiden Hot-pot

This is a very old dish said to date from 1574. The story goes that, during the war between the Dutch and Spanish, a group of hungry young boys found this unusual stew in a big cast-iron pot in an abandoned Spanish garrison after their city, Leiden, had been liberated. In those days of course, there were no potatoes and a type of white bean was probably used instead. Most Dutch families eat *Hutspot* at least once in the winter.

---

1 lb rib steak or stewing beef
1 1/2 lb carrots
1/2 lb onions
2 lb potatoes
salt and black pepper
pat of butter

Bring 4 cups of salted water to a boil in a large pan. Place the meat in the water and leave it to simmer for 1 1/2 hours. Meanwhile, cut the onions and carrots into rings and dice the potatoes. Add to the meat. Leave to simmer, covered, for another 1/2 hour. Remove the meat. Mash the carrots, onions and potatoes together with salt to taste, lots of freshly-ground black pepper and a pat of butter. Place the meat back on top of the vegetables and serve.

Blinde Vinken

Meat Rolls

Veal is eaten widely in Holland and this is a particularly good way of cooking it. This dish should always be served with spring vegetables and it's also delicious with *Spinazie met Soldaatjes* (see page 35).

---

4 thin veal escalopes 4 oz each
4 oz minced veal
salt and freshly-ground black pepper
2 tsp parsley, finely chopped
2 tsp grated shallot or small onion
I tbsp lemon juice or dry white wine
$^1/_2$ cup butter

Season each escalope. Mix the minced veal with salt, pepper, finely-chopped parsley, and the grated onion. With wet hands divide the mince mixture into 4 and form rolls. Place each roll on an escalope. Roll up and secure each escalope with a tooth-pick. Fry the rolls in butter on a high heat until brown, then lower heat. Slowly add the lemon juice or white wine with a little water. Leave the rolls to simmer for another $^1/_2$ hour. Serve with vegetables.

Spinazie met Soldaatjes

Spinach with Little Soldiers

Spinach, rich in vitamin C and carotene, came to Holland in the fourteenth century and has been on the menu ever since. It is best eaten in spring when the spinach is young. Spinach and *Blinde Vinken* (see page 32) are a particularly good combination.

---

4 lb spinach
4 tbsp toasted bread-crumbs
pinch salt
pat of butter
pinch nutmeg
a few drops lemon juice
2 slices white bread
2 hard-boiled eggs

Clean and wash the spinach thoroughly. Cook in a little water for 10 minutes, then drain. Cut or chop the spinach very finely and drain again. Mix with the toasted bread-crumbs, salt, and butter. Add the nutmeg and a few drops of lemon juice to taste. Cut the bread into strips and fry in butter until crisp. Slice the hard-boiled eggs. Turn the cooked spinach into a serving dish and decorate with the strips of fried bread and the egg slices.

Hete Bliksem

Hot Thunderbolt

The Dutch like many types of hot-pot dishes. This is one of the very old sweet-and-sour dishes which have come down from mother to daughter through the centuries. The name *Hete Bliksem* means "hearty fare" and the dish comes originally from the region around Utrecht, in the middle of Holland. Traditionally, fruit was often used in the winter as substitute for vegetables.

---

1 lb cooking apples
1 lb dessert apples
2 lb potatoes
1 lb smoked bacon
salt
1 tsp sugar

Boil the bacon for about 30 minutes in 4 cups of water. Peel, quarter and core the dessert apples. Add to the bacon and cook for $1/2$ hour. Peel and quarter the potatoes and cooking apples. Place the potatoes then the cooking apples on top of the bacon and dessert apples. Add salt to taste and 1 tsp of sugar. Cook until the potatoes are done then remove the bacon. Mash the potatoes and apples. Dice the cooked bacon and stir through the potato and apple mixture. Serve with pork sausages or pork chops.

Prei met Ham Schotel

Leek and Ham Dish

A great variety of vegetables is available in Holland. There are many ways of cooking them including a combination with meat like this leek and ham dish which is cooked all in one dish and is very easy to make. You can use chicory instead of leeks.

2 lb leeks	**White sauce**
1 tsp red wine vinegar	1 tbsp plain flour
salt and pepper	3 tbsp butter
4 oz cooked ham, sliced	2 cups milk
1 cup white sauce	pinch salt
1 cup mature	pinch white pepper
Gouda cheese, grated	pinch nutmeg

Clean the leeks and cut them in 3 inch pieces. Cook for 15 minutes in salted water to which pepper and vinegar have been added. Grease an oval ovenproof dish. Drain the leeks. Roll each leek in a slice of ham and place side by side in the oven dish. Make the white sauce. Melt the butter, stir in the flour, cook for a little, then add the milk slowly, stirring all the time until the sauce is thickened. Add seasonings. Mix the grated cheese in 1 cup of the sauce and pour it over the leeks. Place the oven dish in the middle of a hot oven at 425°F until the top is golden. Serve with rice or mashed potatoes.

Nasi Goreng

Indonesia was one of Holland's colonies for nearly four hundred years and this Indonesian dish has become an integral part of Dutch cooking. It is traditionally on the menu every Wednesday in the Armed Services. It's quick to make but watch out, it's spicy!

I generous cup long grain rice	¹/₂ tsp ground cumin
I leek	2 oz bacon
2 medium onions	8 oz cooked meat
2 cloves garlic	or chicken or prawns
4 tbsp oil	2 tbsp soya sauce
2 tsp sambal oelek	I fried egg per person
(chilli paste)	pickled sliced gherkins,
¹/₂ tsp ground coriander	and tomatoes to garnish

Cook the rice in boiling salted water for 12 minutes. Drain and rinse under cold running water. Peel the onions and chop them finely. Clean the leek and slice finely. Crush the garlic through a garlic press. Fry the onions, leek, garlic, coriander, cumin and *sambal oelek* in the oil until the onions are golden in color. Cut the cooked meat and the bacon in small strips and add to the onion mixture. Add the rice and fry. Stir in the soya sauce. Serve on a big plate, topped with fried eggs, and garnished with sliced gherkins, sliced tomatoes. Serve with peanuts, shrimp crisps and *Zoetzuur* (see page 43) on the side.

Note: If ready-made *sambal oelek* is not available, blend 2 finely-chopped fresh red chillis, ¹/₂ tsp English mustard and I tsp malt vinegar together to make the paste.

Zoetzuur

Pickled Cucumbers

Zoetzuur is typical of the "Jordaan" district of Amsterdam. It is said that the Jordaners would eat *Zoetzuur* on Sunday mornings after a night's drinking to prevent the priests in church from smelling the drink on their breath. Serve it with *Nasi Goreng*, salads, or at parties as a snack.

---

5 large cucumbers
4 cups white wine vinegar
4 cups granulated sugar
8 whole cloves
3 cinnamon sticks
I tsp or 2 pieces whole mace
(makes 4 cups)

Peel and halve the cucumbers lengthwise. Remove the soft seeds. Cut the halves in thin slices. Blanch the cucumbers for I–2 minutes in lightly salted boiling water. Drain well and divide equally over three glass preserving jars placed on a wet tea towel. Boil the vinegar, spices and sugar until the sugar has dissolved. Pour over the cucumbers. After three days pour off the liquid into a pan. Bring the liquid to a boil, cool and pour over the cucumbers again. Seal the jars and keep them in a cool, dark place for a month. The *Zoetzuur* is then ready for eating.

Karnemelkse Pudding met Vanillesaus

Buttermilk Pudding with Vanilla Sauce

This light, refreshing buttermilk pudding is good served as a dessert on a hot summer's day with a delicious vanilla sauce.

Pudding	Vanilla Sauce
4 cups buttermilk	2 cups milk
3 tbsp powdered gelatin	1/2 vanilla pod
1 cup superfine sugar	2 egg yolks
2 lemons	1 1/2 tbsp cornstarch
	3–4 tbsp sugar
	pinch salt

To make the pudding, dissolve the gelatin in 1/2 cup water. Add to the buttermilk and stir. Add the sugar, grated rind of one lemon and the juice of both lemons. Stir until the sugar is totally dissolved. Rinse a pudding basin with cold water and pour the buttermilk mixture into it. Place the pudding in the fridge to set. When ready, turn out on a plate.

To make the sauce, boil half of the milk for the sauce with the vanilla pod and leave to simmer for 10 minutes. Mix the egg yolks, cornstarch, sugar, pinch of salt and the remainder of the milk in a bowl. Add a little bit of the hot milk to the mixture, stirring all the time. Return the mixture to the saucepan with the hot milk and the vanilla pod. Bring the sauce to a boil while stirring. Remove the vanilla pod. Allow the sauce to cool and serve with the pudding.

Limburgse Vlaai

Fruit Flan

Every year as a child I spent some time with relatives in the south of Holland, where I was first introduced to this delicious flan which originates from the province of Limburg. It is usually served at 11 o'clock in the morning with a cup of coffee but it can also be eaten as a dessert.

Dough	Filling
1½ cups plain flour	2 cups dried apricots
4 tbsp melted butter/margarine	1½ tsp arrowroot or cornstarch
1 tbsp dried yeast	½ cup apricot syrup
2 tbsp superfine sugar	1 tbsp apricot brandy
3–4 tbsp lukewarm milk	
½ egg	
pinch salt	

Soak the apricots for several hours in water. Make a smooth yeast dough with the flour, salt, sugar, ½ beaten egg, yeast, milk and melted butter (see method page 4). Cover the dough with a tea towel and leave to rise in a warm place for ¾ hour. Roll out the dough to ¼ inch thick on a floured board and line a greased 10 inch flan dish or pan. Prick the bottom with a fork and leave to rise another ½ hour. Bake the flan for 30 minutes on the bottom of a pre-heated oven at 375°F. When cooked, leave to cool for 10 minutes before removing from the container. To make the filling, cook the apricots gently in a mixture of 1 ¼ cups of water and ½ cup of sugar for 20 minutes. Let it cool. Drain the apricots, reserve the syrup. Arrange the apricots over the cold pastry base to within about 1 inch of the edge. Blend the arrowroot with the apricot syrup and heat gently until thick. Let this glaze cool slightly then brush over the apricots. Decorate the flan with a border of piped whipped cream.

Haagse Bluf

This is a light, fluffy dessert named after the city of The Hague. My apologies to the people from The Hague, but it is said jokingly that this dessert is like them — full of air. While not as substantial as most Dutch desserts, it is really delicious. In this recipe it is made with redcurrant juice, but lemon or orange juice make good substitutes.

---

2 egg whites
³/₄ cup redcurrant juice
¹/₂ cup superfine sugar
6 ladyfingers
(serves 6)

Beat the egg whites together with the redcurrant juice and the sugar until stiff. Divide the *Haagse Bluf* over 6 glass dishes or wine glasses. Insert a ladyfinger in each dish or glass.

Paastulband

Easter Ring

This Easter cake is served after church with a cup of coffee and a dollop of sweetened whipped cream. The cake is placed in the center of a decorated table.

---

3 cups plain flour
³/₄ cup lukewarm milk
1 oz dried yeast
1 egg yolk
5 tbsp soft butter, cut in small pieces
1 oz grated lemon rind
1 tsp salt
2 cups raisins
³/₄ cup sucade or mixed peel
toasted bread-crumbs

Make a smooth yeast dough with the flour, salt, egg yolk, yeast and the milk (see page 4 for method). Add the soft butter pieces and knead. Add the *sucade*, which is a Dutch specialty, or the mixed peel, grated lemon rind and the raisins. Mix well. Shake toasted bread-crumbs into a greased flan ring to cover. Discard any that are loose. Fill the ring with the dough, cover with a tea towel, leave in a warm place to rise for about 1 hour. Bake in the middle of a pre-heated hot oven at 475°F for about 1 hour. Remove from oven and place on a wire rack to cool. When cool, shake some icing sugar through a sieve over the cake. Place a small vase with spring flowers in the middle of the cake ring.

Speculaas

Spicy Cookies

The 6th of December is St. Nicolaas Day. The patron saint of sailors and children, he celebrates his birthday and heralds the start of Dutch Christmas festivities. On the evening before, presents are given to children. For us children it was a very exciting time. The whole family would gather at the grandparents' house. While the presents were handed around, my grandmother served hot chocolate and these spicy cookies.

---

2 cups plain flour
$^1/_2$ tsp baking powder
$1^1/_2$ tbsp speculaas spices (see below)
$^3/_4$ cup light brown superfine sugar
pinch salt
grated rind of a lemon
$^1/_2$ cup almond flakes
$1^1/_2$ tbsp milk
Speculaas Spices
3 tsps cinnamon   1 tsp ground cloves
1 tsp ground nutmeg   1 tsp ground mace

Mix the flour, baking powder, spices, sugar and salt, and lemon rind. Cut the butter through it. Knead this mixture. Add the almonds and milk and knead into a sturdy dough. Leave to rest

voor Saskia

liefs van
Sint & Piet

on a cool place, preferably overnight. Grease a baking sheet. Roll the dough out thinly on a lightly floured surface. Cut out heart, animal or Christmas tree shapes and place on the prepared baking sheet. If you own a *speculaasplank*, press the dough into the well-floured figures. Cut away the dough around them. Knock the cookies carefully out of the board. Place them on the baking sheet. Bake in moderate oven at 350°F for 20 minutes or until golden brown.

Borstplaat

This is a traditional sweet served on the 5th of December, a favorite with both children and adults.

I cup granulated sugar
6 tbsp water
I tbsp butter
I tbsp cocoa powder

Place greaseproof paper on a baking sheet. Grease metal cookie shapes and place on the baking sheet. Continuously stirring, bring sugar, water, cocoa and butter slowly to a boil in a saucepan. Reduce this mixture by boiling until it produces a short thick thread on the rounded side of a spoon. Pour into the greased shapes. Leave to harden and cool. Turn out.

Oliebollen

Doughnuts

Every year, just before New Year's Eve, my mother and grandmother would spend an afternoon in the kitchen cooking these doughnuts. They made buckets full and they were all eaten. *Oliebollen* are traditionally served on New Year's Eve and New Year's Day. This recipe is very old and has been passed on to me by my grandmother.

---

8 cups plain flour
I oz salt
5 eggs
2 oz dried yeast
2 cups lukewarm beer or lager
I cup lukewarm water
3 cups mixed dried fruit (currants, raisins, sultanas)
I cup sucade or mixed peel
5 tangy dessert apples
oil for deep-frying
(makes 80)

Make a smooth yeast batter with the flour, salt, eggs, yeast, water, and beer (see page 11 for method). Add the mixed fruit and peel. Peel and cut the apples in tiny pieces and add to the mixture. Cover the batter with a tea towel and leave to rise on a warm place for about 1 hour. Heat oil in a heavy cast-iron pot. Form a doughnut with 2 well-greased tablespoons and slide into the hot oil. A 10 inch diameter pot will hold

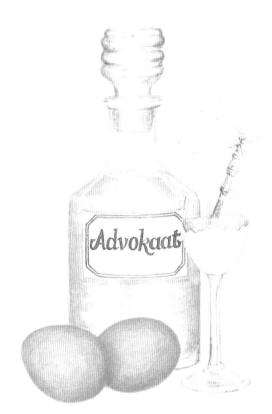

about 6–7 *oliebollen* at the time. After 3 minutes the doughnuts should turn by themselves. If not, just tap them lightly with the spoon and they will turn. Cook them for another 2 minutes. Remove from the oil with a slotted spoon. Drain on kitchen paper then place in a dish. Sieve some confectioner's sugar over them before serving.

Advokaat

I can still remember birthday parties in my grandmother's house when gentlemen were given *Jenever* and the ladies *Advokaat*, served in glasses with a special small spoon. The real *Advokaat* is thick and one eats it instead of drinking it.

---

2 cups Dutch brandy
8 egg yolks
2 cups granulated sugar
$^1/_2$ vanilla pod, seeded

Beat the egg yolks, sugar and the black seeds of vanilla pod in a bowl. To get to the seeds, break the vanilla pod and scrape out the seeds with a pointed knife. Beat the mixture until it is thick, light in color and frothy. Beat the Dutch brandy into it. Place the bowl in a pan with boiling water and beat the mixture until smooth. Do not allow the *Advokaat* to boil. *Advokaat* will stay good for a few months if kept in well-sealed bottles. Serve in a wine glass with a dollop of sweetened whipped cream or poured over ice-cream.

Index